WORDWORKS

WORDWORKS

POETRY ON TELEVISION

EDITED BY NEIL ASTLEY & MARK LAVENDER

BLOODAXE BOOKS

TYNE TEES

ISBN: 1 85224 167 5

First published 1992 by
Bloodaxe Books Ltd,
P.O. Box 1SN,
Newcastle upon Tyne NE99 1SN,
in association with
Tyne Tees Television Limited,
The Television Centre,
City Road,
Newcastle upon Tyne NE1 2AL.

Bloodaxe Books Ltd acknowledges the help
and cooperation of Tyne Tees Television Limited
in publishing this book.

Bloodaxe Books Ltd also acknowledges
the financial assistance of Northern Arts.

Cover reproduction by V & H Reprographics, Newcastle upon Tyne.

Cover printing by J. Thomson Colour Printers Ltd, Glasgow.

Printed in Great Britain by
Bell & Bain Limited, Glasgow, Scotland.

WORDWORKS

LIGHTING CAMERAMAN	Dave Dixon
SOUND RECORDISTS	Nic Grant
	Chris Watson
UNIT ELECTRICIANS	Alan Sharp
	Lew Hedley
TITLE MUSIC	John Cook
DESIGNER	Peter Bingemann
PROPERTIES BUYER	Tom Airey
DUBBING MIXER	Charles Heath
VT EDITOR	Kevin Tait
GRAPHIC DESIGNER	Alan Davidson
PRODUCTION ASSISTANTS	Jill Graham
	Margaret Bramley
ON LINE EDITOR	Bernard Helm
EDITORIAL ADVISERS	Neil Astley
	Andrew McAllister
RESEARCHERS	Marion Tighe
	Ed Gray
PRODUCER	Mark Lavender
DIRECTOR	Rob Cowley
FIRST TRANSMISSION	Tyne Tees Television, May-June 1992
FIRST PUBLICATION	Bloodaxe Books, May 1992

ACKNOWLEDGEMENTS

Acknowledgements are due to the following authors and publishers for permission to publish the poems in this anthology:

FLEUR ADCOCK: for 'Street Song' from *Selected Poems* (Oxford University Press, 1983); SIMON ARMITAGE: for 'Ten Pence Story' from *Zoom!* (Bloodaxe Books, 1989); GEORGE CHARLTON: for 'Nightshift Workers' and 'Sea Coal' from *Nightshift Workers* (Bloodaxe Books, 1989); BRENDAN CLEARY: for 'The Exchange Visit' from *Crack* (Echo Room Press, 1990); DAVID CONSTANTINE: for 'As our bloods separate', 'The Pitman's Garden' and 'Boy Finds Tramp Dead' from *Selected Poems* (Bloodaxe Books, 1991); CAROL ANN DUFFY: for 'Education for Leisure' from *Standing Female Nude* (Anvil Press Poetry, 1985) and 'Poet for Our Times' and 'The Act of Imagination' from *The Other Country* (Anvil Press Poetry, 1990); PAUL DURCAN: for 'Tullamore Poetry Recital' and 'Paul' from *Daddy, Daddy* (Blackstaff Press, 1990); LINDA FRANCE: for 'On the Circle Line' and 'Imaginary Landscape with Real Horse' from *Red* (Bloodaxe Books, 1992); JACKIE KAY: for 'Dance of the Cherry Blossom' from *The Adoption Papers* (Bloodaxe Books, 1991); BRENDAN KENNELLY: for 'Poem from a Three Year Old' and 'A Glimpse of Starlings' from *A Time for Voices: Selected Poems 1960-1990* (Bloodaxe Books, 1990); MICHAEL LONGLEY: for 'The Linen Industry' and 'Weather' from *Poems 1963-1983* (Salamander Press/Gallery Press, 1985); JILL MAUGHAN: for 'Hill End' from *Ghosts at four o'clock* (Bloodaxe Books, 1986); GLYN MAXWELL: for 'Sport Story of a Winner' from *Out of the Rain* (Bloodaxe Books, 1992) and 'Riddle with Answer'; SEAN O'BRIEN: for 'Cousin Coat' from *The Frighteners* (Bloodaxe Books, 1987); TOM PICKARD: for 'The Devil's Destroying Angel Exploded' from *Hero Dust: New & Selected Poems* (Allison & Busby, 1979); JO SHAPCOTT: for 'The Mad Cow Goes Shopping' from *Phrase Book* (Oxford University Press, 1992); KEN SMITH: for 'Eli's Poem' from *The Poet Reclining: Selected Poems 1962-1980* (Bloodaxe Books, 1982) and 'Of Things to Come' and 'Yuppie Love' from *The heart, the border* (Bloodaxe Books, 1990); ANNE STEVENSON: for 'After the End of It' and 'Willow Song' from *Selected Poems 1956-1986* (Oxford University Press, 1987); BENJAMIN ZEPHANIAH: for 'Money' from *City Psalms* (Bloodaxe Books, 1992).

The photographs in *Wordworks* are by: Norman Stafford/Tyne Tees Television (pages 18, 32, 35, 41, 48, 49, plus front cover), Susan Butler (58), Moira Conway (16, 45, 59), Marti Friedlander (50), Ian Ground (56), David Hunter (24), Ingrid Pollard (61), Irene Reddish (43), Joanna Voit (27), and Trevor A. Wallace (37).

CONTENTS

FOREWORD

A few hundred years ago, Sir Philip Sidney, a gentle, brave person, an elegant poet and a firm critic, said that poetry was 'a speaking picture'. *Speaking Pictures* might well have been the title of this book with its varied and vigorous collection of poems by men and women from different cultures and places. The term 'Speaking Pictures' is true in a double sense; first, in the sense that each poem is itself an articulate image; and second, that the images on the screen work both with and against the images in the poems in a startling and revealing way.

Perhaps the core of this fascinating series is the visual and aural vitality generated by the relationships between the poem-images and the screen-images. This relationship can take the form of co-operation in which the spoken line is fortified and amplified by an image that strikes the viewer as being determined to work *with* the line, to make its rhythm more explicit, its passion more expressive. Fleur Adcock's *Street Song* is a case in point: the names of the streets roll off the poet's tongue with almost beguiling harmony; we are inclined to relax into this lyrical litany of street names, and then the images of darkness, the falls into unexpected pits of horrible nightmare shade, the sudden infernos, send a shudder through the viewer, a shudder already suggested by certain words and phrases such as 'he wants to play peculiar games'. This shuddering experience comes to a climax of horror with the poet's admonition to women concerning the presence of Jack the Ripper in the hearts of different men.

> Wear flat shoes, and be ready to run:
> remember, sisters, there's more than one.

These words seem to become, at this stage, part of one's visual experience of the poem; sound becomes image, image becomes sound, to achieve a really powerful effect.

Another good example of image working with image occurs in the poem *Money* by Benjamin Zephaniah. Here, the poet advances down a city street, his body in rhythm with his words, his words a mesmeric music evoking the power, character, influence and presence of money. His face, his hands, his body, the entire street he's passing through, become utterly at one with the poem itself, which is inexorable and hypnotic, a spellbinding evocation of the moneyed universe. A young woman of eighteen or nineteen watched this poem with me; as it unfolded, she got up from her seat and danced with the words, seeming to take them in her arms, dancing joyously,

9

exultantly with them around the room in a hotel by the sea in Ireland. As image cooperated with image, poet with words, words with street movements and viewer's mental dance, the poem achieved a kind of cosmic harmony that proved increasingly irresistible. Many of the poems in this video-series, in this book, have a similar power of barrier-breaking and sympathy-making.

Then there are poems in which the screen images seem to be in a state of fertile conflict with the poem-images. *Eli's Poem*, brilliantly read by Ken Smith, seems to me to be a good example of this. 'I married a crazy woman for her brown hair' and 'I cool her with water' and 'She's out on a hill, wailing' Smith says with painful urgency. But where is she? Where is this woman? In the moon? In the waves? In the shadows? Along the sea coast, somewhere? Astray in his head? Then we begin to realise she's both nowhere and everywhere, a life-absence, a dream-presence, a wraith, a mad reality, a maddening possibility. The screen-images seem to go out of their way *not* to help us, *not* to make helpful and revealing connections, and for a while we are frustrated, strangely lost; then we see, gradually, that this strangely lost, groping, questioning, frenetic atmosphere of disconnection is the essence of the dream-world, more precisely the nightmare-world evoked by Ken Smith. He has given shape to what seemed shapeless, order to what seemed chaotic; and the images in fertile conflict have helped him to achieve this.

Various kinds of television techniques are used effectively to bring out the life in these poems. In George Charlton's moving *Nightshift Workers*, the workers' physical exhaustion gradually affecting their mental state is depicted by a technique of deliberate distortion; faces seem to fall apart; but since it is part of Charlton's design to celebrate the workers' ability to survive and endure, the dislocation is carried out only up to a point, the point at which sheer resolution and normal courage combine to keep these quietly heroic workers intact and coherent.

Carol Ann Duffy's *Poet for Our Times* is set in a kind of tabloid Parnassus with headlines looming at us like manic planets in some futuristic film. Her final line celebrating 'The instant tits and bottom line of art' gets into poetic form and on to the telly screen the daily obsession of certain papers with sex. Duffy's poem is a lively, bouncing, bitter, exhuberant outburst, nicely controlled, crustily read. She makes an aesthetic out of vulgar sensationalism. A performance striking for its gruff integrity.

Poets who are valued for, among other things, their subtlety would not, you might think, come across immediately on screen.

10

But poets like Anne Stevenson, Michael Longley, David Constantine and Jo Shapcott prove that they have the power to be immediate and dramatic as well as subtle and controlled. Longley's *The Linen Industry*, a remarkable love-poem ('what's passion but a battering of stubborn stalks?'), is one of the most hauntingly performed poems of all. It has a majesty all its own. And I shall long remember Jo Shapcott strolling through the supermarket, making the Mad Cow make those hard choices that help to keep humans longer in their prime. Shapcott's sharp intelligence thrills through the images.

That little screen so familiar to us all can be a very daring place. It seems to challenge poets too. But what is a poet if not daring?

Here, at least, the poets have, in their different ways, risen to the challenge. Paul Durcan's daring reading of his poems, the drama of his voice, his eyes, his mouth, his entire face and presence, his odd yet oddly apt intonation and stress, make for a fascinating event. Wizardry and comedy mingle in his words; slapstick and subtlety rub shoulders and noses and eyebrows. I find him mesmeric and funny. His contribution is outstanding.

So, in different ways, are the poems by Sean O'Brien and Tom Pickard. Both these writers conjure up a whole society with few words. They have strong, honest voices. Their compassion is rigorous and real.

Simon Armitage claims that nobody has written of a ten pence piece as well as he. He's right. His final image of the coin being flipped in Wembley's centre circle connects this poem in my mind with Glyn Maxwell's *Sport Story of a Winner*. Anyone who has ever loved a sport or sportsman or sportswoman will love this. Anyone who has saddened at the downfall of sporting genius will sadden here.

Is it absurd to say that one can *see* a voice? See the colours, smiles, frowns, twists and wrinkles of a voice?

I seem to have both seen and heard the voices of these poets. Linda France has a measured but intense voice, like her face. In her voice, passion flows through calculation, calculation measures passion. Brendan Cleary's Northern Ireland accent sounds bittersweet and looks cheeky in Czechoslovakia where he reads 'Kafka in the original'; Jill Maughan's *Hill End* creates an icy cold in her voice, or her voice creates an icy cold in *Hill End*; she has a voice like the winter of 1962. Something of the sea can be seen and heard in George Charlton's voice speaking *Sea Coal*; and Jackie Kay's voice telling us of two men dying of AIDS – 'He thinks I gave it to him' and 'I think he gave it to me' – is a startlingly effective instrument.

11

She has a voice like a long quarrel. The clinical nature of many of the images in the Kay poem *Dance of the Cherry Blossom* brings out the suspicious, stricken humanity of the piece which is terrifyingly close to the battered heart of our age.

Poetry doesn't always work on the small screen. Some of the poems here work better than others. Occasionally, the cooperative images are too explicit and this lessens the impact of both. Part of the value of the viewing experience is to stimulate viewers into asking why it is that certain poems claim your attention in an urgent way while others are less compelling. What are the sources of this compulsion? What intensifies it? What diminishes it? The impressive variety, the intrinsic vitality of the poems that follow here will stimulate a good deal of interesting discussion among readers and viewers alike. The young woman who danced as she watched and heard *Money* being spoken/chanted/half-sung/half-danced by Benjamin Zephaniah advancing in rhythmic revelation down that street told me that, until that moment, she hadn't much interest in verse of any kind. She has now.

BRENDAN KENNELLY

WORDWORKS

'Poetry is life distilled.'
GWENDOLYN BROOKS

PROGRAMME ONE

CAROL ANN DUFFY

'During the last decade, no one would argue seriously with the fact that more people read tabloid journalism than poetry. The poem *Poet for Our Times* uses real headlines from real newspapers, the *Sun*, *Mirror*, *Sport*, etc, to reflect, not entirely seriously, on that situation.'

Poet for Our Times

I write the headlines for a Daily Paper.
It's just a knack one's born with all-right-Squire.
You do not have to be an educator,
just bang the words down like they're screaming *Fire!*
CECIL-KEAYS ROW SHOCK TELLS EYETIE WAITER.
ENGLAND FAN CALLS WHINGEING FROG A LIAR.

Cheers. Thing is, you've got to grab attention
with just one phrase as punters rush on by.
I've made mistakes too numerous to mention,
so now we print the buggers inches high.
TOP MP PANTIE ROMP INCREASES TENSION.
RENT BOY: ROCK STAR PAID ME WELL TO LIE.

I like to think that I'm a sort of poet
for our times. My shout. Know what I mean?
I've got a special talent and I show it
in punchy haikus featuring the Queen.
DIPLOMAT IN BED WITH SERBO-CROAT.
EASTENDERS' BONKING SHOCK IS WELL-OBSCENE.

Of course, these days, there's not the sense of panic
you got a few years back. What with the box
et cet. I wish I'd been around when the Titanic
sank. To headline that, mate, would've been the tops.
SEE PAGE 3 TODAY GENTS THEY'RE GIGANTIC.
KINNOCK-BASHER MAGGIE PULLS OUT STOPS.

And, yes, I have a dream – make that a scotch, ta –
that kids will know my headlines off by heart.
IMMIGRANTS FLOOD IN CLAIMS HEATHROW WATCHER.
GREEN PARTY WOMAN IS A NIGHTCLUB TART.
The poems of the decade...*Stuff 'em! Gotcha!*
The instant tits and bottom line of art.

GEORGE CHARLTON

'This poem charts the process by which continuous physical exhaustion becomes an aspect of mentality. How, with night shift work, people's lives are set apart from the norm. The poem is also a celebration of people's ability to endure such conditions.'

Nightshift Workers

They have come from a factory
Where fluorescent strips flared all night

And ears grew numb to machinery.
They are going home to working wives,

To cooling beds at breakfast time,
Undressing fatigue from their skin like clothes.

15

Later to wake at four and taste teeth
Soft as fur in their mouths.

They live in a dislocation of hours
Inside-out like socks pulled on in darkness

Waking when the day is over.
They are always at an ebb, unlike others

Going out to work in the morning
Where sun and moon shine in the sky together.

SIMON ARMITAGE

'This is the autobiographical life history of a ten pence piece. I thought this
was a highly original idea for a poem until it was pointed out that nearly
everybody has done this at one time or other, mainly as a writing exercise,
mainly at infant school, but never as well as this!'

Ten Pence Story

Out of the melting pot, into the mint;
next news I was loose change for a Leeds pimp,
burning a hole in his skin-tight pocket
till he tipped a busker by the precinct.

Not the most ceremonious release
for a fresh faced coin still cutting its teeth.
But that's my point: if you're poorly bartered
you're scuppered before you've even started.

My lowest ebb was a seven month spell
spent head down in a stagnant wishing well,
half eclipsed by an oxidised tuppence
which impressed me with its green circumference.

When they fished me out I made a few phone calls,
fed a few meters, hung round the pool halls.
I slotted in well, but all that vending
blunted my edges and did my head in.

Once, I came within an ace of the end
on the stern of a North Sea ferry, when
some half-cut, ham-fisted cockney tossed me
up into the air and almost dropped me

and every transaction flashed before me
like a time lapse autobiography.
Now, just the thought of travel by water
lifts the serrations around my border.

Some day I know I'll be bagged up and sent
to that knacker's yard for the over spent
to be broken, boiled, unmade and replaced,
for my metals to go their separate ways...

which is sad. All coins have dreams. Some castings
from my own batch, I recall, were hatching
an exchange plan on the foreign market
and some inside jobs on one arm bandits.

My own ambition? Well, that was simple:
to be flipped in Wembley's centre circle,
to twist, to turn, to hang like a planet,
to touch down on that emerald carpet.

Those with faith in the system say 'don't quit,
bide your time, if you're worth it you'll make it.'
But I was robbed, I was badly tendered.
I could have scored. I could have contended.

17

SEAN O'BRIEN

'This poem, *Cousin Coat*, uses a secret, immortal overcoat to try to make history present. It deals with the obligation to remember the facts, to recognise them in yourself and to know where your loyalties lie.'

Cousin Coat

You are my secret coat. You're never dry.
You wear the weight and stink of black canals.
Malodorous companion, we know why
It's taken me so long to see we're pals,
To learn why my acquaintance never sniff
Or send me notes to say I stink of stiff.

But you don't talk, historical bespoke.
You must be worn, be intimate as skin,
And though I never lived what you invoke,
At birth I was already buttoned in.
Your clammy itch became my atmosphere,
An air made half of anger, half of fear.

And what you are is what I tried to shed
In libraries with Donne and Henry James.
You're here to hear a message from the dead
Whose history's dishonoured with their names.
You mean the North, the poor, and troopers sent
To shoot down those who showed their discontent.

No comfort there for comfy meliorists
Grown weepy over Jarrow photographs.
No comfort when the poor the state enlists
Parade before their fathers' cenotaphs.
No comfort when the strikers all go back
To see which twenty thousand get the sack.

Be with me when they cauterise the facts
Be with me to the bottom of the page,
Insisting on what history exacts.
Be memory, be conscience, will and rage,
And keep me cold and honest, cousin coat,
So if I lie, I'll know you're at my throat.

GLYN MAXWELL

'Here is a tale of sporting prowess, no particular sport, but one followed by
millions. No particular sportsman, but one nationally beloved. The poem
is spoken in the voice of a nation that in falling for him, is falling again for
an old illusion.'

Sport Story of a Winner

He was a great ambassador for the game.
                     He had a simple name.
His name was known in households other than ours.
                     But we knew other stars.
We could recall as many finalists
                     as many panellists.
But when they said this was his Waterloo,
                     we said it was ours too.

His native village claimed him as its own,
                        as did his native town,
adopted city and preferred retreat.
                        So did our own street.
When his brave back was up against the wall,
                        our televisions all
got us shouting, and that did the trick.
                        Pretty damn quick.

His colours were his secret, and his warm-up
                        raindance, and his time up
Flagfell in the Hook District, and his diet
                        of herbal ice, and his quiet
day-to-day existence, and his training,
                        and never once explaining
his secret was his secret too, and his book,
                        and what on earth he took

that meant-to-be-magic night in mid-November.
                        You must remember.
His game crumbled, he saw something somewhere.
                        He pointed over there.
The referees soothed him, had to hold things up.
                        The ribbons on the Cup
were all his colour, but the Romanoff
                        sadly tugged them off.

We saw it coming, didn't we. We knew
                        something he didn't know.
It wasn't the first time a lad was shown
                        basically bone.
Another one will come, and he'll do better.
                        I see him now – he'll set a
never-to-be-beaten time that'll last forever!
                        Won't he. Trevor.

WORDWORKS

'Poets are the unacknowledged legislators
of the world.'

PERCY BYSSHE SHELLEY

PROGRAMME TWO

BENJAMIN ZEPHANIAH

'This is a poem about a hobby I think most people have in common...collecting money. It's got a wonderful title. It's called *Money*.'

Money

Money mek a rich man feel like a big man
It mek a poor man feel like a hooligan
A one parent family feels like a ruffian
An dose who have it won't give yu anything,
Money meks yu friends become yu enemies
Yu start see tings very superficially
Yu life is lived very artificially
Unlike dose who live in poverty.
Money inflates yu ego
But money brings yu down
Money causes problems anywea money is found,
Food is what we need, food is necessary,
Let me grow my food
An mek dem eat dem money.

Money meks a singer singaloada crap
Money keeps horses running round de track
Money meks marriages and money meks divorce
Money meks a student tink about de course,
Money meks commercials
Commercials mek money
If yu don't hav money yu just watch more TV,
Money can save us
Still we feel doomed,
Plenty money burns in a nuclear mushroom.
Money can't mek yu happy
Money can't help yu when yu die,
And dose who hav it continually live a lie.
Children a dying
Spies a spying
Refugees a fleeing
Politicians a lying,
An deals are done
An webs are spun
Loans keep de Third World on de run,
An de bredda feels betta dan dis bredda next door
Cause dis bredda's got money, but de bredda's got more
An de bredda tinks dis bredda's not a bredda cause he's poor
So dis bredda kills de odder
Dat is economic war.

Economic war, economic war,
It may not be de East an de West any more
But de North an de South
Third World fall out
Sugar an oil is what it's about
Economic war, economic war,
Shots fired from de Stock Market floor,
So we work fe a living, how we try
An we try,
Wid so little time fe chilling
Like we living a lie.

Money meks a dream become reality
Money meks real life like a fantasy
Money has a habit of going to de head
I have some fe a rainy day underneath me bed,

Money problems mek it hard fe relax
Money meks it difficult fe get down to de facts
Money meks yu worship vanity an lies
Money is a drug wid legal eyes

Money made me gu out an rob
Den it made me gu looking fe a job,
Money made de nurse an de doctor emigrate
Money buys friends yu luv to hate,
Money made slavery seem all right
Money brought de Bible an de Bible shone de light,
Victory to de penniless at grassroots sources
We come to mash down market forces,
We come to mash down market forces.

JO SHAPCOTT

'The Mad Cow is the heroine of a number of my poems. She's a tragi-comic figure, more wise than fool, in fact her very existence gives her insight into the world, because of the truth of her situation. She is disturbing, disruptive, especially when she comments on society, and I can't help remembering that women who are in any way special, clever or extrovert are often called *You Mad Cow*.'

The Mad Cow Goes Shopping

I approved of it heartily, the multiway underwired bra
from the Pearls Collection in lots of nonstandard sizes.
I took it to try. Next groceries, and maybe a plant or two,
something green and exotic enough to refresh my system,
to help me imagine the reality of the place off-shore
where I recently stashed my savings. You could
exchange it too, the multiwaybra, if it didn't fit:
a serious life or time consideration. I am mostly
vegetarian and skitter up the supermarket aisles
pursuing my health. What goes in that basket is important.
I like it to be from the country, something that had a green
and happy life once, that knew hope and had a generous
and juicy nature. You can't make deals with your stomach
about the future. I try to avoid this craze and that craze
but if you're going to delay death and stay in your prime
week in week out you have to make the hard choices
of the supermarket. Salivating over the loin chops
in the freezer and still passing by equates with goodness
or at least good sense which is the nearest we can get to it
at this time, halving the odds on immediate decay, keeping
a firm straight back well into middle age, the signal
that you want something badly or want something badly not
to happen, because should it happen you're never ready
these days, days of oils, marks and time.

CAROL ANN DUFFY

'The poem *Education for Leisure* was written after a writer-in-residency I had in a very tough comprehensive school. The poem is in the voice of a 15 year old boy, who had little or no literacy. And perhaps, as an act of attention seeking, he was getting involved in acts of violence or near violence.'

Education for Leisure

Today I am going to kill something. Anything.
I have had enough of being ignored and today
I am going to play God. It is an ordinary day,
a sort of grey with boredom stirring in the streets.

I squash a fly against the window with my thumb.
We did that at school. Shakespeare. It was in
another language and now the fly is in another language.
I breathe out talent on the glass to write my name.

I am a genius. I could be anything at all, with half
the chance. But today I am going to change the world.
Something's world. The cat avoids me. The cat
knows I am a genius and has hidden itself.

I pour the goldfish down the bog. I pull the chain.
I see that it is good. The budgie is panicking.
Once a fortnight, I walk the two miles into town
for signing on. They don't appreciate my autograph.

There is nothing left to kill. I dial the radio
and tell the man he's talking to a superstar.
He cuts me off. I get our bread-knife and go out.
The pavements glitter suddenly. I touch your arm.

TOM PICKARD

'This poem was written in the late sixties, at a time of high unemployment, and in despair at the seeming lethargy of organised labour. I was living in Gateshead, unemployed myself, with a young family. My father had recently died, so in a way it is both a personal and a political poem.'

The Devil's Destroying Angel Exploded

no sound
but horns of southern ships
and flapping wings

no colour
but dancing black

producers of heat
confused in the cold

moon full above the dole

sleep children of chilled night
        whose fathers were black men

            sleep bairns
        shivva now
            ya fatha's gold is stolen

strong fathers of a harsh past
    despondent now
slag faces rot against the dole

your hands held hammers
and demanded much
        the moment passed
and bairns curled cad in the womb

worried troops and churches
    you suffocated in the Durham bishop's stables
when Londonderry's jails were full

        the coal you hewed
could have burnt them alive

    instead you begged another shilling

and you made them rich
with killing dust

you should have thrown it in their faces like a bomb
        fed your children joyful stories of the blood of those
        who cheat us

    where we live
shattered smiles break
    on haggard faces

manufacturers of filth
    marry our wealth
in a confetti of votes

            no breath of slum air

councillor elected by my father
   he said you wore a worker's cap
called everybody *marra*
   but the word I heard was slave

   bloodfluke in the brain of an ant
that gold chain was scraped
   from the lungs of pitmen

     your gown is a union leader
gutted and reversed

      look dozy fathers look
your masters have changed
drawn by the river mist
    you drift in a dream

   ah father your flesh is overrun with lice
and all your life you nurtured many parasites

KEN SMITH

'These two pieces are about urban renewal and the replacement of the derelict and the old by the new and the young and the upwardly thrusting and the upwardly mobile. So we all end up one day living in a heritage museum.'

Of Things to Come

Down the Bendy Road to Cyprus and Custom House
where the new cities rise from the drawing-boards
and the ghosts-to-be of George in his Capri,
JoJo in her birthday suit drinking white wine with soda
fly in from Paris for the weekend. Later
they'll gather with friends by the marina.
Later they'll appreciate the view of the river.
Later they'll jive to the mean mad dance of money
between the tower blocks over the runway
amongst the yachts already moored in the development.

Yuppie Love

What he calls her: my little pocket calculator
my fully portable my VDU my organiser my mouse
oh my filofax my cellnet my daisywheel.

What he dreams driving home at the wheel
on the brimming motorway: her electronics
the green screen of her underwear her digital display.

Oh my spreadsheet he groans in the night:
my modem my cursor lusting after her floppies
wanting her printout her linkup her entire database.

WORDWORKS

'Poetry is what makes the invisible appear.'
NATHALIE SARRAUTE

PROGRAMME THREE

LINDA FRANCE

'Fairly regularly I have dreams about train journeys and tunnels, stations and missed connections. Freud, who was so eager to relate practically everything to sex, would have been in his element analysing these dreams of mine. After waking from one of these dreams, I wrote this poem.'

On the Circle Line

If Freud was right concerning trains in dreams,
Why is mine always in the wrong station?
If, in bed, all is not what it seems,
Why's it so hard to resist temptation?

It's easy to guess the derivation
Of his hypothesis, his phallic themes;
But it's still open to arbitration
If Freud was right concerning trains in dreams.

But I wake myself up with primal screams
When I find I've got no reservation.
When I can see how the iron horse steams,
Why is mine always in the wrong station?

An excellent means of transportation,
Even though it may take you to extremes;
But is it worth all the aggravation
If, in bed, all is not what it seems?

I'm not the sort of person who esteems
A snail's trail – life without titivation.
Right this minute I could write reams and reams
Why it's so hard to resist temptation.

Whatever the nocturnal assignation,
Between the sheets, or in my day-time dreams,
I can't ignore the implication
Of the tannoy voice announcing it seems
That Freud was right...

CAROL ANN DUFFY

'It occurred to me that although poets cannot pass laws as politicians can, there is nothing to stop them so doing in their imagination. In *The Act of Imagination* I have compiled a quite personal list of things that are too awful even to think about. Under the Act, the following things may be prosecuted for appalling the imagination.'

The Act of Imagination

Ten More Years.
A dog playing Beethoven's 'Moonlight Sonata'.
President Quayle.

The pyjamas of Tax Inspectors.
The Beef Tapeworm (*Taenia Saginata*).
British Rail.

Picking someone else's nose.
The Repatriation Charter.
Gaol.

The men. The Crucifix. The nails.

The sound of the neighbours having sex.
The Hanging Lobby.
The Bomb.

Glow-in-the-dark Durex.
A Hubby.
Bedtime with Nancy and Ron.

The sweet smell of success.
A camel's jobby.
On

and on. And on. And on.

Eating the weakest survivor.
A small hard lump.
Drinking meths.

Going as Lady Godiva.
A parachute jump.
One breast.

Homeless and down to a fiver.
A hump.
Bad breath.

Here is a space to fill in things you suggest.

Death.

BRENDAN CLEARY

'I wrote *The Exchange Visit* a few years ago when I was staying in Ireland. It's a strange poem. I'm not really sure I know what it means, but in some way it explores the relationship between one's private life and the public world outside...I think...'

The Exchange Visit

well I woke up this morning
& i was in Czechoslovakia
a peaceful suburb of Prague
to be exact

it had rained
so the lawns all glittered
& i had a splitting head
from too much 80% vodka
well presumably so

the whole thing is a mystery
because now i talk the language
i have a Czech wife
three handsome healthy Czech children
(for the moment their names escape me)
a Czech house with a Czech roof
overlooking a Czech swimming pool

what luxury!

it's really quite some existence
i've had carved out for myself
& i've read Kafka in the original
& all my old favourites like Philip Marlowe
in handy pocket-size Czech translations

still i have a job remembering
how i fell asleep
beneath the shadow
of the lame cow
at the edge of Mulligan's field
in the drizzle
in the breezes whirling tractor blades
in the old sod

GLYN MAXWELL

'The riddle is a very ancient English verse form. This one blazes a false trail parallel to the correct answer, so the poem is in effect a double entendre. Traditionally, the answer was not given at the end of a poem, but then the Anglo-Saxons probably had a longer attention span than you do.'

Riddle with Answer

What am I. Dangerous at the top,
Tall and straight. When standing up
A vital and strong thing, when down
Insignificant. When alone
Changing nothing. In a room,
Admired by fools and kids, I seem
All potential, part of a plan.
In attendance. Ready when.
A queen's inflicted jealousies
Will see me in her enemies
Either after or during. I
Provoke a silence or a sigh.
Either way a problem. What
I start I finish. What you get

You see and see again too late.
I am release. I can be hate,
I separate. When I'm the bride's
I enter to the dark insides
But ain't no progenitor. Not on your life.
I'm in this hand. Pen? Knife.

PAUL DURCAN

Tullamore Poetry Recital

It was a one-man show in Tullamore,
'The Sonnets of Shakespeare'.
The newspaper advertisement bubbled:
'Bring Your Own Knitting.'
The audience of twenty-five
Was devout, polite, attentive,
All with their knitting,
Men and women alike with their knitting.
I shut my eyes and glimpsed
Between the tidal breakers of iambic pentameter
The knitting needles flashing like the oars of Odysseus.

But as the evening wore on, and the centuries passed,
And the meditations, and the thanksgivings,
And darkness fell, and with it a fullish moon,
Not quite full but fullish,
Putting on weight by the teaspoonful,
One was aware of a reversal advancing,
Of incoming tides being dragged backwards.
The knitting needles were no longer oars
But fiddles in orchestras sawing to halts.
One became aware of one's own silence.
One was no longer where one thought one was.
One was alone in the pit of oneself, knitting needles.

WORDWORKS

'Poetry is truth seen with passion.'
W.B. YEATS

PROGRAMME FOUR

MICHAEL LONGLEY

'This poem derives its images from the processes involved in the manufacture of linen: pulling up the flax, building it into stooks, laying it out in dams to rot the fibres away from the grass stems, and then, when the material had been woven, laying it out in fields so that at the height of summer when it was bleaching in the sun it would seem that there'd been a fall of snow.'

The Linen Industry

Pulling up flax after the blue flowers have fallen
And laying our handfuls in the peaty water
To rot those grasses to the bone, or building stooks
That recall the skirts of an invisible dancer,

We become a part of the linen industry
And follow its processes to the grubby town
Where fields are compacted into window-boxes
And there is little room among the big machines.

But even in our attic under the skylight
We make love on a bleach green, the whole meadow
Draped with material turning white in the sun
As though snow reluctant to melt were our attire.

What's passion but a battering of stubborn stalks,
Then a gentle combing out of fibres like hair
And a weaving of these into christening robes,
Into garments for a marriage or funeral?

Since it's like a bereavement once the labour's done
To find ourselves last workers in a dying trade,
Let flax be our matchmaker, our undertaker,
The provider of sheets for whatever the bed –

And be shy of your breasts in the presence of death,
Say that you look more beautiful in linen
Wearing white petticoats, the bow on your bodice
A butterfly attending the embroidered flowers.

PAUL DURCAN

Paul

In the rush-hour traffic outside the centre-city church
I stood with my bicycle waiting for the lights to change –
A Raleigh bicycle with upright handlebars
That I had purchased for two pounds fifty pence in The Pearl –
When a priest in black soutane and white surplice
Materialised in the darkness of the porch.
He glided over to me:
'I am about to begin a funeral Mass but I have no mourners.
Would you be prepared to act as a mourner for me?'

As we paced up the aisle, the priest enlightened me:
'He was about the same age as yourself,
All we know about him is that his name was Paul.'

I knelt in the front pew,
The coffin on trestles alongside me,
Its flat abdomen next to my skull.
I felt as a mother must feel
All alone in the maternity ward

With her infant in the cot at the foot of the bed,
A feeling that everything is going to be all right
But that we are all aliens in the cupboard,
All coat hangers in the universe.

The priest – a seven-foot-tall, silver-haired peasant in his eighties –
Instructed me to put my bicycle in the hearse beside the coffin.
The two of us sat in the front with the driver.
At a major traffic junction near the cemetery of Mount Prospect
We had to brake to avoid knocking down a small boy.
The car behind us bumped into our rear bumper,
Inducing the bicycle to bump against the coffin.
We saw a prominent politician in the back seat blessing herself.
At the graveside as the priest said prayers
I got the feeling that the coffin was empty;
That Paul, whoever he was,
Was somewhere else.

'How do you know that his name was Paul?'
I asked the priest as we tiptoed away.
He handed me a creased sheet
Of blue vellum unlined notepaper – Belvedere Bond:
Dear Paul – Thank you for your marriage proposal
But I am engaged to be married in Rome in June.
Best wishes always, Mary

Queen of Loneliness.

JILL MAUGHAN

'*Hill End* is about a double parting. Not only is it about the end of love but
it is also about the leaving of a much loved house. I attempted to mirror
the sadness and vulnerability of the couple and the loneliness of the scarred
landscape.'

Hill End

If our coming was a spring, then our going is well caught
in this biting season, though our small embrace
meets poorly with the features of this vast, moorland face,
with its voice as penetrating as a raging, windy day,

and its hill top snow like the white hair on a wise man's head.
But the stone wall lines that cut like secateurs
tell of a kind of inextractable pain, walking here with you,
crossing these icy patches, and even in our knowing

we have a hundred miles to go and a lifetime, none of this
compares to what is wrought in the iron stare of this place.
Our years are hardly a graze on this skin and our
energy almost a trespass on this living silence.

But our purpose as much as our past is breathing
on the haunting road of this familiar route,
and is breathing too, in the house at the end of the hill,
which is "sold" and to which we will not return.

DAVID CONSTANTINE

'This poem has a traditional topic, transience. The lovers attempt to escape
from transience by, so to speak, taking themselves out of it; by taking them-
selves out of time, they form a ring against time. The central image of the
poems is that of a clock, a clock pecking away, pecking away at their lives.'

'As our bloods separate'

As our bloods separate the clock resumes,
I hear the wind again as our hearts quieten.
We were a ring: the clock ticked round us
For that time and the wind was deflected.

The clock pecks everything to the bone.
The wind enters through the broken eyes
Of houses and through their wide mouths
And scatters the ashes from the hearth.

Sleep. Do not let go my hand.

KEN SMITH

'This poem was a unique gift in that I dreamt that I was reading it in a book, and reading it in the dream I realised I was dreaming and so I memorised it, woke up and wrote it down. Now it exists in a book, *Eli's Poem*.'

Eli's Poem

I met a woman from the sea coast,
she took me aside in the bushes
and wrapped me around and said *we are alone*
as the moon up there is with just two sides.
I did what was to be done and came away with her.
Now I am with a crazy woman
who hurts herself with ashes and briars
running in the scrub. She takes blankets
and stuffs them under her skirt for a child.

She takes out the blanket and croons on it,
washes it, beats it with sticks till it cries
and tears it to pieces. Her lament
goes down the street on cut feet in the gravel.
She runs in a nightgown thinking she's the police
and charges anyone with ridiculous crimes
like wearing a hat sideways and walking wrong.
The people here know her and smile and say
yes they will come to the court to answer.
She writes everything down in her book.
In bed she's like trying to catch a hare.
She wants to sleep with me all night
till my back breaks, if I doze off
she wakes me crying for love.
I married a crazy woman for her brown hair.
At first I thought she was pregnant
but her blood runs, the doctor shakes his head at me.
I tell her your child is in the other country
and will not come here because of your frenzy.
She runs to the church crying she's evil,
the priest holds out his god's battered arms
and says *come child everyone's evil*.
I cool her with my breath, I cool her with water.
She's insatiable as the river, like winds
she has no place to go and runs
from whatever does not move. She's holding a wooden knife
and staring it down till it becomes pure menace
and I fear it myself. I sleep with her
because then I control her and know where she is,
but I don't know what runs in her.
Now she is out on the hill wailing
cutting her flesh on the stiff grass
where I go to her lamenting.

WORDWORKS

'A poet's hope: to be,
like some valley cheese,
local, but prized elsewhere.'

W.H. AUDEN

PROGRAMME FIVE

MICHAEL LONGLEY

'This poem turns inside out the usual perspectives of closeness and distance. Brookweed, by the way, is a tiny white flower, small enough to be enclosed by a raindrop.'

Weather

I carry indoors
Two circles of blue sky,
Splinters of sunlight
As spring water tilts
And my buckets, heavy

Under the pressure of
Enormous atmospheres,
Two lakes and the islands
Enlarging constantly,
Tug at my shoulders, or,

With a wet sky low as
The ceiling, I shelter
Landmarks, keep track of
Animals, all the birds
In a reduced outdoors

And open my windows,
The wings of dragonflies
Hung from an alder cone,
A raindrop enclosing
Brookweed's five petals.

GEORGE CHARLTON

'This poem plays on a contrast that coal, which once brought prosperity to our region and power to the nation, has now left both in decline – although it's not the coal's fault.'

Sea Coal

This is the coal coast. Where Easington stops
Splintered suns float on the North Sea's pressure
Compounding best coal squeezed from strata

Between seafloor and rockbed. Below,
Sunken eyes lie back exhausted;
Cold currents unpick the sinews of men

Who rippled in earnest, coaling Imperial flotillas:
Both bone-cage and bulkhead fronds
Have fossilised in sea-salt.

Underwater siftings are washing
From the stokehold of the sea, poor nuts,
For sea coal burns badly, gives off meagre heat.

It has become derelict treasure salvaged
Out of an undertow. Coal has produced
Its own decay: coal-pickers who scrounge

Bent-backed on the water-fringe, balance
Sacks on the cross-bars of clapped-out bikes,
Stretch their spines and look out gazing –

There dead things have come from the sea to tell
Bleached tales to the hard-up and out of work,
Rumouring of desolation riding the slack.

FLEUR ADCOCK

'I wrote this poem when I was living in Newcastle in 1979 at the time of the Yorkshire Ripper. There was a theory that he might actually come from somewhere closer to here than Yorkshire, so I thought I would write a kind of sinister nursery rhyme, using the quaint names of the city streets, but with this figure lurking among them. Just before I finished it, they arrested him, but I think it's still relevant.'

Street Song

Pink Lane, Strawberry Lane, Pudding Chare:
someone is waiting, I don't know where;
hiding among the nursery names,
he wants to play peculiar games.

In Leazes Terrace or Leazes Park
someone is loitering in the dark,
feeling the giggles rise in his throat
and fingering something under his coat.

He could be sidling along Forth Lane
to stop some girl from catching her train,
or stalking the grounds of the RVI
to see if a student nurse goes by.

In Belle Grove Terrace or Fountain Row
or Hunter's Road he's raring to go –
unless he's the quiet shape you'll meet
on the cobbles in Back Stowell Street.

Monk Street, Friars Street, Gallowgate
are better avoided when it's late.
Even in Sandhill and the Side
there are shadows where a man could hide.

So don't go lightly along Darn Crook
because the Ripper's been brought to book.
Wear flat shoes, and be ready to run:
remember, sisters, there's more than one.

DAVID CONSTANTINE

'I was asked to write a poem about a garden, and remembered an allotment in a ruined chapel by a scrapyard. The juxtaposition fascinated me, and in the poem I tried to develop its possibilities.'

The Pitman's Garden

Man called Teddy had a garden in
The ruins of Mary Magdalen
By Baxter's Scrap. Grew leeks. What leeks need is
Plenty of shite and sunshine. Sunshine's His
Who gave His only begotten Son to give
Or not but shite is up to us who live
On bread and meat and veg and every day
While Baxter fished along the motorway
For write-offs Teddy arrived with bags of it
From home, which knackered him, the pit
Having blacked his lungs. But Baxter towed in wrecks
On their hind-legs with dolls and busted specs
And things down backs of seats still in and pressed
Them into oxo cubes and Teddy addressed
His ranks of strapping lads and begged them grow
Bonnier and bonnier. Before the show
For fear of slashers he made his bed up there
Above the pubs, coughing on the night air,
Like the Good Shepherd Teddy lay
Under the stars, hearing the motorway,
Hearing perhaps the concentrated lives
Of family cars in Baxter's iron hives.
Heard Baxter's dog howl like a coyote
And sang to his leeks 'Nearer my God to Thee'.
He lays his bearded beauties out. Nothing
On him is so firm and white, but he can bring
These for a common broth and eat his portion.

Leaving town, heading for the M1,
Watch out for the pitman's little garden in
The ruined fold of Mary Magdalen.

ANNE STEVENSON

'I moved to Langley Park, until recently a Durham mining village, the summer my friend, the poet Frances Horovitz, was dying of cancer. *Willow Song* names the flowers on the coal mine's grave: a song for Frances, a lament for times past, an intimation of continuing life.'

Willow Song

I went down to the railway
But the railway wasn't there.
A long scar lay across the waste
Bound up with vetch and maidenhair
And birdsfoot trefoils everywhere.
But the clover and the sweet hay,
The cranesbill and the yarrow
Were as nothing to the rose bay
    the rose bay, the rose bay,
As nothing to the rose bay willow.

I went down to the river
But the river wasn't there.
A hill of slag lay in its course
With pennycress and cocklebur
And thistles bristling with fur.
But ragweed, dock and bitter may
And hawkbit in the hollow
Were as nothing to the rose bay,
    the rose bay, the rose bay,
As nothing to the rose bay willow.

I went down to find my love,
My sweet love wasn't there.
A shadow stole into her place
And spoiled the loosestrife of her hair
And counselled me to pick despair.
Old elder and young honesty
Turned ashen, but their sorrow
Was as nothing to the rose bay
    the rose bay, the rose bay,
As nothing to the rose bay willow.

LINDA FRANCE

'The title of this poem echoes the American poet Marianne Moore's exhortation that poetry should present "imaginary gardens with real toads in them". She also said that "there are things that are important beyond all this fiddle. Reading it, however, with a perfect contempt for it, one discovers in it after all, a place for the genuine." In my poem I'm trying to capture a genuine response to a genuine horse and ride with it through the landscape of my imagination.'

Imaginary Landscape with Real Horse

Imagine the blur of day turning into grey
evening, dusk lowering its soft pad on the land,

still river – a deep wash of essential blue, grey,
submerged jade. Then this shock of white, static

marble. Each step nearer pulses its own echo
of white – dream; mirror; flesh. Horse. She walks

across the floating paddock, rolling her fetlocks.
The great black globe of her eye hurls itself

right to the heart of me. And all I'm saying
is *Horse!* stroking her boned cheek, her bold trust.

I want to climb the fence, and her; ride
bareback over the hills, all one with laughing,

this crisp close night, its intimate moon
and few fresh stars; a female centaur shot from

the arrow of earth on the verge of spring.
This snorting creature takes my breath away.

And gives it back: our aspirations,
airy wildness mingling.

WORDWORKS

'Personal relations are the important thing
for ever and ever.'

E.M. FORSTER

PROGRAMME SIX

BRENDAN KENNELLY

'One night my three-year-old daughter wouldn't sleep so I brought her down to the kitchen and there was a vase full of flowers and the petals were falling from the flowers. She asked me a lot of questions about the petals, so I explained to her that the flowers were dying, and she began to think about people dying, and so the questions poured out of her.'

Poem from a Three Year Old

And will the flowers die?

And will the people die?

And every day do you grow old, do I
grow old, no I'm not old, do
flowers grow old?

Old things – do you throw them out?

Do you throw old people out?

And how you know a flower that's old?

The petals fall, the petals fall from flowers,
and do the petals fall from people too,
every day more petals fall until the
floor where I like to play I
want to play is covered with old
flowers and people all the same
together lying there with petals fallen
on the dirty floor I want to play
the floor you come and sweep
with the huge broom.

The dirt you sweep, what happens that,
what happens all the dirt you sweep
from flowers and people? Is all the
dirt what's left of flowers and
people, all the dirt there in a
heap under the huge broom that
sweeps everything away?

Why you work so hard, why brush
and sweep to make a heap of dirt?
And who will bring new flowers?
And who will bring new people? Who will
bring new flowers to put in water
where no petals fall on to the
floor where I would like to
play? Who will bring new flowers
that will not hang their heads
like tired old people wanting sleep?
Who will bring new flowers that
do not split and shrivel every
day? And if we have new flowers,
will we have new people too to
keep the flowers alive and give
them water?

And will the new young flowers die?

And will the new young people die?

And why?

ANNE STEVENSON

'A love affair gone wrong leaves an aftertaste of bitterness that can be as powerful as love itself. *After the End of It* is a poem about the raw painfulness of parting.'

After the End of It

You gave and gave,
and now you say you're poor.
I'm in your debt, you say,
and there's no way to repay you
but by my giving more.

Your pound of flesh is what you must have?
Here's what I've saved.

This sip of wine is yours,
this sieve of laughter. Yours,
too, these broken haloes
from my cigarette, these coals
that flicker when the salt wind howls
and the letter box blinks like a loud
eyelid over the empty floor.

I'll send this, too, this gale between rains,
this wild day. Its cold so cold

I want to break it into panes
like new ice on a pond; then pay it
pain by pain to your account.
Let it freeze us both into some numb country!
Giving and taking might be the same there.
A future of measurement and blame
gone in a few bitter minutes.

DAVID CONSTANTINE

'Towards Christmas some years ago I saw this headline in a newspaper: BOY FINDS TRAMP DEAD. In those days I had a lot to do with the lives of homeless people, and I can vouch for the details recorded here, fantastic though some of them may seem.'

Boy Finds Tramp Dead

But for your comfort, child, who found him curled
With crizzled cheeks, his hands in his own ice,
Among the trapped dead birds and scraps of girls,

His spectacles and broken teeth put by
Along the window with a pile of pence,
Remember this man was the son of nobody,

Father, brother, husband, lover, friend
Of nobody, and so by dying alone
With rats hurt nobody. Perhaps he joined

And mended easily with death between
Newspaper sheets in drink and did not wake
Too soon, at midnight, crying to sleep again,

Alive and hung on cold, beyond the embrace
Of morning, the warm-handed. He was pressed
Together when you found him, child, but names

Had left his lips of wicked men released
Quickly in sunlight and of one who baked
Asleep inside a kiln and many at rest

With cancer in the casual ward or knocked
Under fast wheels. These be conjured with
To Christ as instances of mercy, being racked

Himself on boards beside a prolapsed hearth.
His vermin died. The morning's broken glass
And brightening air could not pick up his breath.

Little by little everything in him froze,
Everything stopped: the blood in the heart's ways,
The spittle in his mouth, his tongue, his voice.

BRENDAN KENNELLY

'My father and mother were married for nearly fifty years. The day she
died he began to die. This poem is about him on a typical morning of his
grief visiting my brother's house, where I am staying, expecting my father.'

A Glimpse of Starlings

I expect him any minute now although
He's dead. I know he has been talking
All night to his own dead and now
In the first heart-breaking light of morning
He is struggling into his clothes,
Sipping a cup of tea, fingering a bit of bread,
Eating a small photograph with his eyes.

The questions bang and rattle in his head
Like doors and cannisters the night of a storm.
He doesn't know why his days finished like this
Daylight is as hard to swallow as food
Love is a crumb all of him hungers for.
I can hear the drag of his feet on the concrete path
The close explosion of his smoker's cough
The slow turn of the Yale key in the lock
The door opening to let him in
To what looks like release from what feels like pain
And over his shoulder a glimpse of starlings
Suddenly lifted over field, road and river
Like a fist of black dust pitched in the wind.

JACKIE KAY

'This is a poem about two men who are dying of AIDS, both at the same time. It was motivated by the death of a friend of mine. I just felt how awful it must be to be dying at the same time as your lover.'

Dance of the Cherry Blossom

Both of us are getting worse
Neither knows who had it first

He thinks I gave it to him
I think he gave it to me

61

Nights chasing clues where
One memory runs into another like dye.

Both of us are getting worse
I know I'm wasting precious time

But who did he meet between
May 87 and March 89.

I feel his breath on my back
A slow climb into himself then out.

In the morning it all seems different
Neither knows who had it first

We eat breakfast together – newspapers
And silence except for the slow slurp of tea

This companionship is better than anything
He thinks I gave it to him.

By lunchtime we're fighting over some petty thing
He tells me I've lost my sense of humour

I tell him I'm not Glaswegian
You all think death is a joke

It's not funny. I'm dying for Christ's sake
I think he gave it to me.

Just think he says it's every couple's dream
I won't have to wait for you up there

I'll have you night after night – your glorious legs
Your strong hard belly, your kissable cheeks

I cry when he says things like that
My shoulders cave in, my breathing trapped

Do you think you have a corner on dying
You self-pitying wretch, pathetic queen.

He pushes me; we roll on the floor like whirlwind;
When we are done in, our lips find each other

We touch soft as breeze, caress the small parts
Rocking back and forth, his arms become mine

There's nothing outside but the noise of the wind
The cherry blossom's dance through the night.

BIOGRAPHICAL NOTES

Fleur Adcock was born in 1934 in New Zealand. She has published eight poetry books with Oxford University Press, including *Selected Poems* (1983), *The Incident Book* (1986) and *Time-Zones* (1991), and four with Bloodaxe, including *The Virgin & the Nightingale* (1983) and *Hotspur* (1986).

Simon Armitage was born in 1963 in Huddersfield. He works as a probation officer. His first collection *Zoom!* (Bloodaxe, 1989) was a Poetry Book Society Choice, and was shortlisted for the Whitbread Prize. His latest books are *Xanadu: a poem-film for television* (Bloodaxe, 1992) and *Kid* (Faber, 1992).

George Charlton was born in 1950 in Gateshead. He is a lecturer at Newcastle College. In 1984 he was joint winner of the *Evening Chronicle* Poetry Competition. His first collection, *Nightshift Workers*, was published by Bloodaxe in 1989; a second book, *City of Dog*, is forthcoming.

Brendan Cleary was born in 1958 in Co. Antrim, Northern Ireland. He edits the magazine *The Echo Room*, lives in Newcastle, and works as a part-time lecturer and performance poet. His publications include *White Bread & ITV: Selected Poems 1984-1990* (Wide Skirt Press, 1990).

David Constantine was born in 1944 in Salford. He is Fellow in German at the Queen's College, Oxford. He has published seven books with Bloodaxe, including *Selected Poems* (1991), a novel, *Davies* (1985), and translations of Friedrich Hölderlin (1990) and Henri Michaux (1992).

Carol Ann Duffy was born in 1955 in Glasgow. She is a freelance writer, and lives in London. She has published three award-winning collections with Anvil Press: *Standing Female Nude* (1985), *Selling Manhattan* (1987) and *The Other Country* (1990).

Paul Durcan was born in 1944 in Dublin. His recent collections are published by Blackstaff Press: *The Selected Paul Durcan* (1982), *The Berlin Wall Café* (1985), *Going Home to Russia* (1987) and *Daddy, Daddy* (1990), the last of which won the Whitbread Poetry Prize. His latest book is *Crazy About Women* (National Gallery of Ireland, 1991).

Linda France was born in 1958 in Newcastle. She lives in the North Tyne valley, and works as a part-time tutor in adult education. She won the Basil Bunting Award in 1988 and 1989. Her first book of poems is *Red* (Bloodaxe, 1992).

Jackie Kay was born in 1961 in Edinburgh, and grew up in Glasgow. Her first collection, *The Adoption Papers* (Bloodaxe, 1991), was shortlisted for the *Mail on Sunday* / John Llewellyn Rhys Prize, and won a Scottish Arts Council Book Award. She lives in London.

Brendan Kennelly was born in 1936 in Co. Kerry, Ireland. He is Professor of Modern Literature at Trinity College, Dublin, and has published over 20 books, including *The Penguin Book of Irish Verse*, and four books with Bloodaxe: *Cromwell* (1987), *A Time for Voices: Selected Poems 1960-1990* (1990), *Medea* (1991), and the number one Irish bestseller *The Book of Judas* (1991).

Michael Longley was born in 1939 in Belfast. He has published six books of poems, most recently *Gorse Fires* (Secker, 1991), winner of the Whitbread Poetry Prize. His *Poems 1963-1983*, originally published in paperback by Penguin, is being reissued by Secker as *Smoke in the Branches*.

Jill Maughan was born in 1958 in Newcastle, and lives in Co. Durham. In 1984 she was joint winner of the *Evening Chronicle* Poetry Competition with her poem 'Hill End'. Her first collection, *Ghosts at four o'clock*, was published by Bloodaxe in 1986, and her children's novel, *The Deceivers*, by Collins in 1990.

Glyn Maxwell was born in 1962 in Welwyn Garden City. His first collection, *Tale of the Mayor's Son* (Bloodaxe, 1990), was a Poetry Book Society Choice, and was shortlisted for the *Mail on Sunday* / John Llewellyn Rhys Prize and the *Sunday Times* Young Writer's Award. His second collection, *Out of the Rain* (Bloodaxe, 1992), is a Poetry Book Society Recommendation.

Sean O'Brien was born in 1952 in London, grew up in Hull, and now lives in Newcastle. He has published three collections: *The Indoor Park* (Bloodaxe, 1983), *The Frighteners* (Bloodaxe, 1987) and *HMS Glasshouse* (Oxford University Press, 1991).

Tom Pickard was born in 1946 in Newcastle, left school at 14, and set up Morden Tower poetry readings with Connie Pickard in Newcastle in 1964. His books include four poetry collections, a novel, a history of the Jarrow March, and *We Make Ships* (Secker, 1989), a portrait of shipbuilding on the Wear. He is a freelance writer and film-maker.

Jo Shapcott was born in 1953 in London. She is the only writer to have won first prize in the National Poetry Competition twice – in 1985 and 1991. Her poetry collections are *Electroplating the Baby* (Bloodaxe, 1988) and *Phrase Book* (Oxford University Press, 1992).

Ken Smith was born in 1938 in North Yorkshire. He was writer-in-residence at Wormwood Scrubs for two years, and has published books on prisons and Berlin. His poetry books are published by Bloodaxe, including *The Poet Reclining: Selected Poems 1962-1980* (1982), *Terra* (1986), *Wormwood* (1987) and *The heart, the border* (1990).

Anne Stevenson was born in 1933 in Cambridge of American parents, and grew up in the States. She has published several poetry books with Oxford University Press, including a *Selected Poems* in 1987. *Bitter Fame*, her biography of Sylvia Plath, was published by Viking in 1989.

Benjamin Zephaniah was born in 1958 in Birmingham, and grew up in England and Jamaica. He is one of Britain's best-known rap poets, and has released several records. His books include *The Dread Affair* (Arena, 1985) and *City Psalms* (Bloodaxe, 1992).

Galloway Shipwrecks.

The Sinking
of the
SS MAIN

By

Peter C. Miller

Sunquest

i

Copyright © Peter C Miller 2014

ISBN 978-0-9519115-4-9

Published and Printed by:
Sunquest
Ardwell,
Stranraer,
Wigtownshire, DG9 9LX
Scotland.

Front Cover:
Picture of the SS MAIN sunk in Luce Bay.

Introduction

This booklet is a spin off from my book "Galloway Shipwrecks", published in 1992.

As this year of 2014 marks the centenary of the start of World War One, I decided to write the full story of the sinking of the Steam Ship MAIN. The audacity of this incident brought the war fully home to the people of Wigtownshire.

Although I wrote an account of the loss of the MAIN in my book; in the years since its publication, much more information has come to light.

Therefore, this book is a dedication to all those lost during this terrible conflict; especially to the men of the Mercantile Marine, many who gave their lives attempting to maintain the essential supply of goods and equipment to where they were needed.

I use the story of this small ship to highlight the horror and stress these sailors experienced on a daily basis, never knowing when or where they would be attacked.

I also take this opportunity to mention and thank Mr. Malcolm J Hill for his invaluable help with further information, which allowed me to fill some of the gaps in the original account. Also my thanks go to Mrs. Sue Ware who, ten years ago, sent me a copy of Captain Robert McCorquodale's statement of events leading to the loss of his ship and crew.

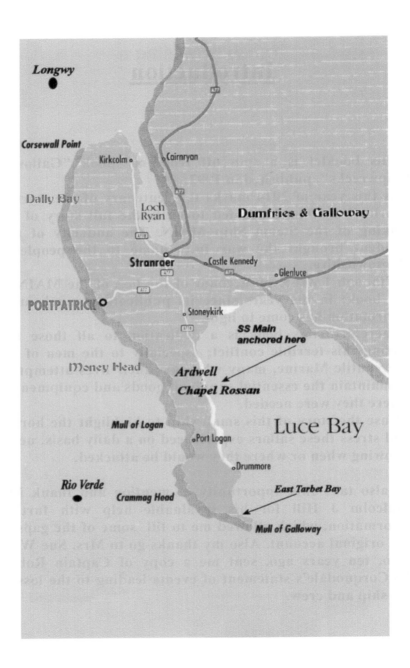

The Sinking of the SS MAIN

Chapter One.
The Attack.

Logan Estate Factor Henry Michie awoke with a start, not knowing what had disturbed his slumber, he listened but all he could hear was the wind and rain lashing against his bedroom window.

Lying staring at the window, trying to get back to sleep, he suddenly became aware of brief distant flashes of light followed by a series of bangs and rumbles. Henry thought he had the answer to his rude awakening, putting it down to thunder and lightning. Settling down he was soon fast asleep; totally unaware of the terrible tragedy that had just taken place out in the bay, not far from his house at Chapel Rossan.

It was the 8th. of October 1917 and the SS MAIN had just finished discharging her cargo of coal at Belfast. Captain McCorquodale was not looking forward to the voyage to Liverpool as he had worked out that they would be clearing Belfast Lough at around 5pm that afternoon which meant he would be going against the ebb tide. On top of that, a strong N.W wind was forecast which was not good, even though she was in ballast, she was still riding high; with wind against tide it was going to be an uncomfortable trip, to say the least. The only consolation was, that when they reached Liverpool, his vessel was due to have a refit and his crew could have some well earned shore time.

The MAIN got under way at 3pm; heading down the Lough into an already freshening wind, Captain McCorquodale turned to his First Mate, who had taken the wheel, and said "well Thomas, this is a favourable breeze at the moment, I trust it doesn't strengthen". However, his hopes were dashed, for by 8pm the wind and sea had steadily increased, so he decided to run for shelter.

Making for the Scottish coast the MAIN rounded the Mull of Galloway at about 10pm, out of the worst of the weather. The night was pitch black so they steamed slowly up Luce Bay for just about 10 miles, making for Chapel Rossan Bay near the small village of Ardwell, where Captain McCorquodale reckoned they would get the best shelter from the storm.

Having spent some time laying mines off Liverpool Bay, the German submarine UC 75 set a course north; running on the surface as much as possible but forced to submerge and use her electric motors for some of the time,. She was a UC11 class U-boat of 410 tons displacement surfaced, with a length of 165ft and 17ft. beam. As well as her electric motors she had two 6 cylinder diesel engines; was capable of 11.8 knots surfaced and 7.3 knots submerged with a dive depth of 160 ft. (50m). Armed with 18 mines,7 torpedoes and a 88mm KL/30 deck gun,with a crew of 26.

Although he would be very close to the RN Airship Station at East Freugh; Commander, Oberleutnant Johannes Lohs; because of the stormy weather and dark night, decided to put into Luce Bay for shelter. Arriving in East Tarbet Bay, under the Mull of Galloway just before 10pm. he took advantage of the shelter to transfer torpedoes from the outside storage containers and reload whilst recharging batteries.

UC75 had only been in the bay a short time, when the conning tower lookout thought he heard the engine of a vessel approaching quite close. He quickly notified the officer of the watch, who called the captain. The gun crew were put on standby for action stations; just able to make out the dimmed lights of a ship, they watched as it steamed slowly by, only a few hundred yards away. Lt. Lohs was not going to miss a chance of sinking another enemy vessel, urged his crew to complete their tasks. At approximately 11.30pm he gave the order to follow the noted course of the steamer; knowing that there was no suitable harbour, he reckoned she must have anchored further up the bay.

Arriving off Chapel Rossan, the MAIN anchored roughly a mile and a half from shore in about seven fathoms. The time was 11.50pm and Captain McCorquodale had been on deck for four hours, the mate took over the watch and the captain went below.

About 1am he returned on deck for a check on the weather; although the barometer was rising, it was still blowing a full gale from the N.N.W. with squally showers. Going to the charthouse he checked their position, the tide was now flooding and pushing the vessel beam into the wind, not ideal for getting some rest.

With the mate, Finnish born Thomas Soderstrom plus one deckhand and a gunner on watch; second engineer William Blair and a fireman on duty, the captain retired to his cabin.

The MAIN was a single screw steamer of 716 gross tons, with accommodation for 14 crew. She was constructed by Muir & Houston, completed by Makie & Thompson on the Clyde at Govan Glasgow for the MAIN Colliery Company Ltd. Registered at Cardiff in 1904, used primarily for shipping coal; she operated from the Neath Abbey Wharves transporting coal mainly to the Irish ports of Dublin, Belfast and Cork and sometimes to Rouen in Northern France.

Some of the crew of the MAIN with Captain McCorquodale and steward Paul August in the foreground.

At the start of the war in 1914, the MAIN was fitted with a single gun on her quarterdeck and carried two Royal Navy Reserve gunners, Leading seaman Gunner John McIver born Stornoway, Isle of Lewis Scotland and Seaman Gunner John McLeod born Kyles Outer Hebrides Scotland.

Meanwhile UC75 was moving very slowly as she searched for the steamer; when around 2am, out of the dark suddenly loomed the blacked out shape of the MAIN; avoidance action was quickly taken, but too late, the net cutter, positioned on the bow, made contact under the stern of the MAIN, scraping against the hull of the anchored vessel.

3

On the MAIN; watchmen, John McLeod and Irish born Able Seaman Edward White were huddled together out of the weather having a smoke, totally oblivious to the impending danger. They may have felt the slight impact when the U-boat touched and chose to ignore it, putting it down to the weather, or even investigating and seeing nothing in the pitch black stormy night, took no action.

However, on UC75, no chances were taken; for all they knew the alarm may have been raised and the MAIN was armed with a 5.7cm (6 pounder) gun. So as the crew came to action stations, the U-boat was manoeuvred into position.

There was no warning given, no offer for the crew to abandon their ship; only a hail of shells, as UC75 opened fire with her 88mm deck gun; at only 200 feet away she couldn't miss, making sure every hit counted. The first shells crashed into the steamers quarterdeck, an obvious target, disabling her gun and bringing down the mast. The U-boat gun crew, who were capable of firing at a rate of 15 to 26 rounds a minute; had to cease their murderous assault, when one of their crew, seaman Rodat, was thrown overboard by the recoil of the gun, so the attack was stopped to facilitate a rescue of the injured man.

Captain McCorquodale, finding it difficult to get to sleep because of the rough weather; had just managed to doze off, when the first shells struck home; he was almost ejected from his bunk as his ship rocked with the impact of the 30lb missiles, A glance at his watch showed 2.30am; he quickly made for the deck.

Another shell hit home, the shrapnel sounding like the rattle of a machine gun as it struck the superstructure, making it impossible for him to leave the doorway. Crouching in the exit he tried to take stock of the situation; shielding his eyes he strained to see, but was unable to make out very much against the driving rain, The squall suddenly passed, giving a brief period of clear sky. Looking in the direction he thought the bombardment was coming from, he made out the unmistakeable shape of a submarine, just off the Port Quarter, so close he could see the gun crew on the deck silhouetted against the clearing sky.

4

By this time the ship had been hit many times and was on fire with smoke and steam filling the air. Suddenly, the gun fell silent and taking advantage he managed to work his way to the starboard side of the vessel; now with some protection he lay low, but the gun was still silent so he headed for the quarterdeck. Coming upon the engineer Blair and gunner Mcleod, he was informed that their gun was useless; taken out with the first salvo of shells.

The rest of the crew had taken full advantage of the lull and launched the port lifeboat, pulling well clear of their stricken vessel; believing, because the second mate Walter Forsch had been killed during the initial attack, the men left behind were either dead or hopefully launching the starboard lifeboat.

Whether the three men, so incensed at being attacked without warning, with one thought, had made their way to the gun deck, in an attempt to retaliate, only to find the gun out of action; we will never know.

Captain McCorquodale certainly noted that the gun was useless so probably took a pragmatic approach; as there was nothing they could do, did not elaborate on the situation in his statement of events. All that remained, was to try and save themselves.

Gunner Mcleod made for the port side and disappeared; the captain and the engineer, managed to launch the starboard boat, only, no sooner had it hit the water it became awash, riddled with shrapnel. The engineer, maybe seeing it as his only option jumped into the half filled boat whilst the captain made back to the port side only to find no sign of the lifeboat or any crew.

On the U-boat the rescue of Seaman Rodat had been successful and he was safely below receiving treatment so the gun crew recommenced firing with its 88mm, at such close range, finished off its deadly task with clinical precision.

Captain McCorquodale, rather than be killed by an exploding shell, leapt into the cold dark rough sea to take his chance with the elements. The MAIN, now well down in the water, was done for and he soon lost sight of her as the U-boats gun once more fell silent.

Luckily the captain managed to make his way to the water filled starboard lifeboat, finding the engineer clinging on for dear life.

The two of them held onto the almost submerged boat, fully aware their chances of survival were not great, when out of the dark appeared the port lifeboat. The crew finding it hard to believe that their captain and engineer were still alive, quickly hauled them aboard but of Gunner McLeod there was no sign, he had obviously perished.

It transpired that during the lull, the lifeboat with nine of the MAINs crew aboard;, had been taken alongside the U-boat and the men questioned. They gave the Germans details of the MAIN; reporting that their captain had been killed along with the rest of the crew, totally unaware the three missing men were still alive aboard the severely damaged ship. They also informed the U-boat captain that the lifeboat was damaged and leaking badly; in spite of this they were cast adrift to fend for themselves. Drifting away on the wild stormy sea; pure luck bringing them upon the two survivors.

Captain McCorquodale tried to ascertain whether all the crew had made it, he could get no sense out of the confusion that prevailed except that Walter Forsch the Second Mate had been killed.

Then Panic took over when someone shouted that the boat was taking water more rapidly, Before some sort of calm could be established, the situation was made even worse when the boat was swamped by a huge wave and began to settle deeper in the water, the sea now breaking right over her. Each time this happened one or more of the now exhausted crew; unable to hold on with frozen fingers, were washed away and lost from sight in the darkness.

Later that day two boys came upon what they thought was a dead body, timidly they approached but jumped back when they saw it move. Overcoming their trepidation they rendered what assistance they could, until more help arrived.

The half dead man proved to be the sole survivor of the murderess attack on the SS MAIN, Captain McCorquodale. Somehow he had managed to get hold of a lifebuoy and after many hours in the cold water had come ashore on the other side of Luce Bay near the village of Portwilliam. Later when the captain had recovered from his ordeal, he put his extraordinary survival down to the fact that being quite a large gentleman, he was well protected against the icy waters and cold wind.

SS MAIN sunk in 7 fathoms.

Possibly UC 75

7

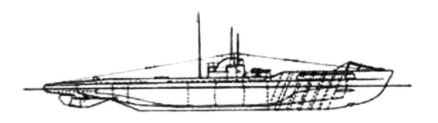

Drawing of a UCII Class U-boat

UC II Class U-boat.
(Note the containers for extra torpedoes on the side and the net cutter on the bow.)

Chapter Two
Aftermath

Captain Robert McCorquodale was a seaman through and through; born 1st of May 1867 in the village of Crarae, on the shore of Loch Fyne Argyllshire Scotland. His father, Donald McCorquodale, who died February 10th. 1896 from a stroke, had also been a Master Mariner, so it was definitely in the blood.

Robert had three brothers, John born 1864, Alex born 29th December 1865 and Archibald born 1868. Three sisters followed, Mary, February 1873, Ann, September 1875 and finally Bessie, born 1878.

John the eldest was soon to follow the call of the sea, in 1881 at the age of 16, he was serving as Ordinary Seaman on board his father's Smack, the "Catherine and Mary" running cargoes on the west coast of Scotland.

Nothing much is known of Roberts early life; by the time he was thirty, he was a Master Mariner and is listed in the 1901 Census as being on board a ship at Monkwearmouth Southwick Sunderland. It transpired that he first served on the MAIN, when it went into service in 1904, as mate to his elder brother Captain John McCorquodale. In 1907 he was to take over command of the MAIN and in the 1911 census, is residing in Cadoxton, Coedffranc, Neath, Glamorganshire.

It was 10 days before the captain recovered enough physically from the event, but mentally he found the loss of his crew and close friends extremely hard to overcome, resulting in a minor breakdown.

Finally he was able to give his account of that terrible night; making a statement was hard, as he had to virtually relive the full horror bit by bit and no doubt relived it many times over the rest of his life. So much so it would be three months before he returned to sea

All twelve crew of the MAIN had perished and over the days immediately following the sinking of the ship, bodies started to be washed ashore. Two were cast up near Portwilliam, Royal Naval Reserve Gunner John McLeod age 39, who never got the chance to fire his gun in defence of his ship and Steward, Paul August age 59. Both men were interred in nearby Mochrum Parish Church yard. A further two bodies, not identified, were found at the head of the bay and buried in Glenluce Old Luce Churchyard.

Vessels sunk by war causes came under the Government's war risks insurance scheme and The Main Colliery Company was given a replacement, a World War 1 C4-class standard coastal cargo ship, Built by W Harkess & Sons of Middlesbrough named the SS War Trees and owned by the Shipping Controller (WW1) London.

She was handed over in 1920; registered at Bristol; renamed "SS Goodwill of Bristol". Captain Robert McCorquodale was given command of the new slightly larger (871 tons) vessel.

In 1922 on a voyage to Antwerp Belgium he was taken ill and died on the 10th, October 1922 in the Civil Hospital Ghent. His body was brought back to the UK; taken to Scotland and buried in Crarae Argyll, his birthplace.

Definitely a canny bachelor scot, he had spent his life and money investing in stocks and shares so when his will was read on the 11th. November 1922 at Crarae Lochfyne, the total amount of his estate amounted to the grand total of £7390.18s.6d (£355,660.01 in today's money-2014) all going to his sister Bessie Sinclair.

A full copy of the captains will is included at the back of this book (Appendix Two).

Bessie married John Sinclair on New Year's Eve 1913 in Glasgow and it seems she was Roberts only living relative, unfortunately Bessie would only enjoy her legacy for a short period, as she sadly died aged 49 on the 11th. November 1927 after an operation for cancer.

Oberleutnant zur See Johannes Lohs, his job done, thought it wise to get as far away as possible from the bay before daylight. Hopefully, the alarm would not be raised for some time but he was fully aware of the possibility of a search for him, if the weather allowed; carried out by airships from the Royal Naval Airship Station at East Freugh.

Leaving the confines of the bay UC 75 headed south and torpedoed a small vessel, the SS W.M. Barkley of 569 tons, carrying a cargo of stout from Dublin to Liverpool. The attack was carried out without warning on the 12th October 1917 with the loss of four lives.
On the 3rd November south of the Isle of Man, the UC 75 attacked the passenger steamer Atlantian (9399 tons) with torpedo, but failed to sink her.
On the 4th November she was back in Scottish waters; off the Wigtownshire coast she came upon the SS Longwy a French ship of 2315 tons, with a cargo of iron ore bound for the Clyde. Yet again without warning, Captain Lohs attacked with torpedo and sank her with the loss of all 26 crew. The bodies of her captain, Joseph Huet and two seamen were washed ashore near Girvan Ayrshire. (See Galloway Shipwrecks).

The reason for adding details of these further actions was to throw some doubt on the accuracy of Lt. Lohs version of events in his official log, during his attack on the SS MAIN. As his report differs quite a bit from Captain McCorquodale's statement. The slight discrepancies in timings, although they more or less coincide; can be explained by the fact that Captain McCorquodale made his statement 10 days after the event when not fully recovered.
Lt. Lohs probably made his log entry whilst trying to clear Luce Bay before daylight, fearing a possible search for him by the airships from the RN Airship Station at East Freugh.

Using both accounts (*See Appendix One*) and a touch of dramatic licence, I have constructed what I believe to be a more accurate picture of the attack, especially as I do not believe that Lt. Lohs when he reports that he allowed the crew to abandon ship <u>before</u> he opened fire.

Mainly because, from February 1917 U-boat commanders were given the go ahead to attack and sink all armed ships without warning as part of the escalation in U-boat activity in a last ditch attempt to bring Britain to its knees.

Lt. Lohs completed his patrol and returned to base where he handed over command of UC75 to Oberleutnant zur See Walter Schmitz who sailed from Flanders at 7pm on May 22, 1918, carrying a crew of 33. After laying his mines, Schmitzt made his way north and cruised around, studying the situation of certain convoys that were expected off Flamborough Head. It was then he encountered the SS Blaydonian, which accidentally struck the submarine casing and forced it to the surface. The small escort destroyer HMS Fairy was close by and immediately raced to the scene; seeing the submarine on the surface, challenged her. After a second challenge went unanswered, Fairy put both engines at half speed and rammed the stern section of UC75.

This was an action to frighten the crew into surrender rather than sink the submarine as there could have been British captives aboard. Some of her crew scrambled out onto the deck and manned the deck gun, firing a shell at the destroyer. Fairy immediately retaliated by firing 40 rounds back at the U-boat and as she turned they went full speed ahead on both engines, ramming the U-boat and fatally damaging it, but the impact with the larger vessel split the Fairy's bow wide open.

Without hesitating, two of the German submariners leapt from the deck casing onto the destroyer's forecastle where they stood with their hands up, surrendering. Twelve others including the commander, who had jumped overboard as the submarine sank, were picked up from the sea. Unfortunately, damage sustained by the destroyer was so severe she sank within an hour of the action.

Lieut. Barnish, captain of the Fairy, was awarded the DSO for his fine effort in protecting the convoy and sinking the UC75. His action had been momentous, in taking out a U-boat that had sank over 125,000 tons of allied shipping; many lives and ships would be saved.

 As for Oberleutnant zur See Johannes Lohs, he took command of UB 57 sinking another 25 ships and damaging 10 before his U-boat struck a mine east of the Straits of Dover on the 14th. October 1918 and was a total loss.

His body was washed ashore a week later and his final resting place is the German cemetery at Ysselsteyn in the Netherlands.

The reported position for the sinking of the MAIN is 1.5 miles East of Drummore? But Captain McCorquodale states in his narrative of events that he steamed 10 miles up Luce Bay and anchored off Chapel Rossan. Also, from the U-boat log, it took well over two hours after leaving East Tarbet Bay at the Mull of Galloway, for UC 75 to locate the MAIN. Confirming Captain McCorquodale's account that he steamed ten miles up the bay, taking around two hours to reach Chapel Rossan.

I, the author of this book, decided to try and prove beyond doubt that the SS MAIN was sunk out off Chapel Rossan Bay near the village of Ardwell. Using the original monochrome photograph of the sunken vessel, I was able to match the landscape shown on the photo, exactly to the topography of coast, straight across from Chapel Rossan.

I took a photo from the shore at Chapel Rossan and printed it on clear film; when overlaid on the original photo the topography matched exactly.

Also, in my original account in "Galloway Shipwrecks", I state that Captain McCorquodale lost his son. This information was given to me during an interview I had with a local man in 1990. He said he was on the beach the morning after the sinking and saw the body, which he was told was the captains son. As there is no record of Captain McCorquodale having a son on board, or even being married, then of course my informant; who was a young boy at the time, was mistaken or confused by another event he may have witnessed. Unfortunately he died a short time after I spoke to him .

The two pictures on the next page are to show the position of the MAIN before she was attacked and of course after she was sunk; although hazy, the skyline matches.

Simulation of SS MAIN anchored off Chapel Rossan Bay
(Looking across Luce Bay from Chapel Rossan)
(Note the skyline between foremast and mainmast, although further
away they do match)

SS MAIN sunk in 7 fathoms.

Chapter Three

The Final Act

The MAIN had been badly damaged, but after the war ended, a survey at the beginning of 1919; carried out by the Ardrossan Salvage Company, revealed it could be possible to salvage her.

So working in conjunction with the ship builders, Messer's Vickers & Sons of Barrow in Furnace; who had developed special inflatable pontoons, each one capable of lifting 100 tons. They decided to test them on raising the SS MAIN from her watery grave.

In the summer of 1919 work began, after preparation work the fully inflated pontoons were secured to the wreck by divers and at dead low water spring tide the cables were tightened; as the tide came in, gradually the MAIN would be lifted off the bottom. This is a simplified description of the "Tidal Lift" operation. Once off the bottom she would have been moved to shallow water until she touched bottom. Every time this happened, they would wait for low water and the whole procedure would start again; cables fully tightened, so as she lifted with the tide, the ship once more could be moved even further into shallow water until it was possible to pump her out.

By the 19th. of August she had been towed to a position off Drummore where work could be carried out patching up the shell damage so she could be fully pumped and cleaned out in preparation for her journey to the shipyard..

During this operation it was reported that human remains were discovered, although not confirmed. It is not inconceivable that the report was true as Walter Forsch the Second Mate had been killed during the initial attack by UC 75. The remains were not, or could not be identified and may be the occupant of the grave to the unknown sailor of the First World War in Kirkmaiden Churchyard!

16

It was to be the summer of 1920 before repairs were completed enough to allow her to be towed to Ardrossan. Meanwhile, whilst a suitable tide was waited for, curious members of the public; for a small charge, were allowed on board. Maybe some of these local visitors needed to have actual physical contact with the wartime incident that had unbelievably taken place, bringing the horrors of war right to their doorstep.

The salvaged SS MAIN lying off Drummore 1919

All donations went towards the erection of a memorial in Kirkmaiden Churchyard Drummore, to not only the lost crew of the SS MAIN but also to sailors lost when the SS Rio Verde was torpedoed by U 100 off Cramag Head on the 21st. February 1918. Followed by the sinking, just two miles away, of the SS Ulabrand by torpedo (U 86) the next day. The bodies of five of those from the Rio Verde were washed ashore and are buried beside the memorial. There were many vessels sunk by enemy action off SW Scotland, with great loss of life, but the attack on the MAIN was one of the more unsavoury in the way it was carried out.

In December 1920 the MAIN was towed to Ardrossan where it was completely renovated and put back into service in 1922; registered at Glasgow with new owners, the Ford Shipping Company Ltd. In 1925 she was sold to the Tyne Tees Steam Shipping Company Ltd. registered at Newcastle on the 16th. February 1926 still as the MAIN, but three days later her name was changed to the MARDEN, as the Managing Director of the company lived in Marden House Whitley Bay Northumberland.

On the 27th. May 1929 the MARDEN was making her way up the North Sea, when off Cromer Knoll Norfolk, she was involved in a collision with   SS THE SULTAN. The MARDEN was fatally damaged and her crew of, ironically thirteen; definitely an unlucky number for the MAIN/MARDEN, this time were safely picked up by THE SULTAN.

The crew of the SS MARDEN

19

Unconfirmed photo of the SS THE SULTAN but it also could be the MAIN or MARDEN?

The Bell from SS MAIN

The "Ships Bell" from the SS MAIN, recovered when the vessel was salvaged. It was used for many years by the owner to call "Time" in his pub in Ayr, Ayrshire, Scotland.

In memory of the crew:

Ture Constantine(Thomas) Soderstrom   Mate.   Age 46
Born Aland Islands, Finland.

Walter Forsch   Second Mate.   Age 36
Born Riga, Latvia.

Charles E Macnair   Engineer.   Age 36
Born Campbeltown Argyll
Scotland.

William Miller Blair   Second Engineer.   Age 26
Born Harrington, Cumberland.

Paul August   Steward.   Age 59
Born Martinique, West Indies.

John McIver   Leading Seaman   Age 32
Born Isle of Lewis   Gunner RNR.
Outer Hebrides Scotland

John McLeod   Seaman Gunner   Age 38
Born Scalpay Isle of Harris.   RNR.

Karl Silman   Able Seaman   Age 39
Born Riga Latvia

Edward Whyte   Able Seaman   Age 34
Born Kilrane, Wexford,Rosslare.

Nils Anderson   Fireman   Age 31
Born Norway

Abdullah Muhammad   Fireman.

Said Abullah   Fireman.

**Graves of two of the crew from the SS MAIN
buried in
Glenluce Old Luce Churchyard.**
(*Unfortunately the month is wrong, should be October*)

**Mocrum Churchyard.Memorial naming two of the crew of the
MAIN,
Paul August and John McLeod.**

The Salvaged SS MAIN lying off Drummore 1919

Appendix One

This is a rough translation of UC-75 Log Book Entry

East Tarbet Bay 8.10.1917

Kept the boat stationary a few hundred metres from land while torpedoes from outside storage containers were moved into the boat and reloaded. While this was going on a steamer entered the bay

1130pm Barometer is rising

Torpedoes have been reloaded There is no harbour in the bay so the steamer must have anchored somewhere

0200 hrs

Too dark to see anything rammed the steamer with our net cutter

0245

Attacked the steamer, which had a gun on the stern, with artillery. Sailor Rodat was thrown overboard by the pressure from the recoil. We managed to fish him out again. He was injured and needs treatment inside the boat. Sunk steamer with gun fire after the crew had abandoned ship.

English ship (he means British) with *5.7cm* gun *MAIN,* 715t from Belfast to Liverpool had taken shelter in the bay due to heavy seas

Survivors told us that the master and 13(possible this was 3) men were killed There were 8 men and helmsman or navigator in the lifeboat The steamer did not manage to defend itself. The steamer sank while at anchor some two miles from land

0615. A vehicle on the shipping route. Course 300 Started to approach. but gave up because it was a small ship of about 1000t Dived because I am already right in front of him

Laid the boat on the sea bed, 38, 42 and 55m

Had a regular look around Sunny, no traffic West wind force 7-8

0715

Surfaced Went to the Irish east coast because the sea was to rough further out

10. 10 -0300

Attacked a steamer, didn't shoot (torpedoes) because it was only 800t. The sea is too rough for using the gun. It is a similar ship to Main.

Captains narrative on the loss of the SS Main 9th. October 1917

Left Belfast about 3pm.October 8th strong breeze from the N.W.

At 8pm with the wind and sea increasing, I decided to make for shelter, rounded Mull of Galloway 10 pm steamed up Luce Bay for about 10 miles, night dark, let go anchor at 11.50 pm at Chapel Rossan in seven fathoms.I was on deck from 8 pm until midnight until I was relieved by the mate, who was taking the watch from midnight until 4am. I went below to my cabin;

I came up on deck again at 1 o'clock to see the state of the weather, no improvement. Then I went into the charthouse, and remained for some time. After coming out I spoke to the mate and gave him some instructions. It was blowing a gale from NW by N and dark. I then retired to my cabin leaving the mate, one deck hand and one gunner on watch, also the second engineer William Blair on duty and one fireman.

At about 2.30 am I suddenly heard shelling close alongside., and what sounded like a machine gun. I at once made for the deck, when I got to the top of the stair, shells were flying past me. This was on the port side (the only exit from the cabin) so that I had to withdraw for a little.

On coming out I saw what appeared to be a submarine on the port quarter about 200ft distant shelling us. At this time there was smoke, steam and fire about. I crossed to the starboard side and made for the gun platform. When I got aft, the engineer and the gunner McCleod immediately told me that the gun was knocked out of action and the rest of the crew were launching the the port lifeboat. this one the gunner also made for.

The engineer and myself launched the starboard lifeboat, but no sooner was it in the water than she was awash riddled with shell, the engineer jumped into her. I remained on deck and went to the port lifeboat, but found that she was then launched and clear. Seeing that the ship was then in a sinking condition I jumped overboard and with a great struggle I managed to get hold of the starboard lifeboat, which was awash, and the engineer hanging on.

Shortly afterwards the port lifeboat (which appeared to me to be floating alright and most of the crew in her) picked up the engineer and myself. I asked if all hands were in the boat but got no definite answer, as there was great confusion, some shouting that the boat was holed and one distinctly called out that the second mate was killed. Shortly after this the boat capsized and the seas washed clean over her.

This happened several times and on each occasion one or more of the crew were lost, failing to secure a hold, until only three were left, who died from exposure in the waterlogged boat and were washed away by the heavy seas, leaving me the sole survivor, who was driven ashore by the force of wind and sea, in an exhausted condition after having been fully 15 hours in the water. Owing to the capsizing of the boat, the rough sea and the dark night, I did not actually see the steamer sink, but From her condition before I jumped overboard, I have no doubt whatever that she sank shortly after we got clear.

<u>Signed:</u>

<u>R Mc Corquodale, Master. October 19. 1917.</u>

.

A 88mm gun as fitted to UC-75.

Appendix Two

Copy of Captain McCorquodale's Will

Compeared Donald MacGregor, Coach Hirer, Oban and Duncan Macdougall, Solicitor, Oban.

who being sworn and examined, **severally** depone , I know the above Deponent and that **she** is the **sister** of the said defunct.

All of which is truth, as the Deponent shall answer to God.

(Signed) DONALD MACGREGOR,
D. MACDOUGALL,
ALEXR. L. MACARTHUR.

Collated by

DUTY £ 1 : 10 : —

I. ESTATE BY ITSELF.			
PARTICULARS	£	s.	D.
Moveables in United Kingdom	42	10	7
Moveables Abroad			
Other Moveables, per Account No. 1			
Heritable Estate, per Account No. 1	175	—	—
TOTAL	217	10	7

II. PROPERTY SETTLED OTHERWISE THAN BY DECEASED'S WILL.			
PARTICULARS	£	s.	D.
Moveable Property, as per Account No. 2			
Heritable Property, as per Account No. 2			
TOTAL	—	—	—

rm 117.

rm for Record
y of Inventory
Personal Estate
m up on Inland
venue Forms
4-1 and A-4.

INVENTORY

OF

THE PERSONAL ESTATE

OF

ROBERT McCORQUODALE, Master Mariner, late of Crarae,
Lochfyne.

DECEASED.

AT Dunoon , the twenty fourth day of November
Nineteen Hundred and twenty two the following Inventory of the Personal
Estate of the late Robert McCorquodale,
was presented for registration in this register, along with Settlement
of the deceased conform to law by R. S. Corrigall,
Solicitor, Dunoon.
Inbentorp of the Moveable or Personal Estate and Effects, wheresoever
situated, of the late Robert McCorquodale, Master Mariner, late
of Crarae, Lochfyne.

who died at the Civil Hospital, Ghent, Belgium,
on the Tenth day of October 1922.

	I. SCOTLAND.	£	s.	D.
1.	Furnishings in room at Crarae, and personal effects estimated value.	25	–	–
2.	On Account Current with Commercial Bank of Scotland Limited, St. Enoch Square, Glasgow.	50	14	9
3.	£100 War Savings Certificate No. 221383 re-payable 2nd. January 1923.	99	5	–
4.	— Do. — No.252478 repayable 12th March 1923.	99	–	–
5.	Moss' Empires Limited 40 Preference Shares at £3:10/-	140	–	–
	Estate in Scotland. £	413	19	8
6.	II ENGLAND. Boots Cash Chemist(Southern) Limited 100 'C' 6% Preference £1 shares @ 19/-	95	–	–
7.	Calico Printers Association Limited 100 5% Preference £1 shares @ 17/-	85	–	–
8.	Bovril Limited 100 7½% Ordinary shares @ 22/6	112	10	–
9.	The Weardale Street, Coal & Coke Company Ltd. 100/-			

28

	100 6% Cumulative Preferred Ordinary shares @ 30/-	100: -: -
10.	Whitbread & Company Limited 1 £4:10/- per cent Preference share of £100	67: -p -
11.	Page & Overtons Brewery Limited £100 4½% First Mortgage Debenture Stock	70: -
12.	Acadia Sugar Refining Company Limited £100 Preference Shares £1 each @ 1/1½	5:12: 6
13.	Scott, Son & Co, Limited @ Cannon Street, London 100 5% Cumulative Preference £1 shares @ 15/-	75: -: -
14.	John Lovebond & Sons Limited, The Brewery, Greenwich £100 4½% First Mort. Debenture Stock.	60: -: -
15.	Wall Paper Manufacturers Limited 100 5% Cumulative Preference Shares @ 17/6	87:10: -
16.	Consolidated Cambrian Limited 100 Preference Shares of £1 each @ 14/-	70: -: -
17.	British & Argentine Meat Company Limited £100 6% Debenture Stock	105: -: -
18.	— Do. — 200 6% Cumulative & P articipating Preference Shares of £1 each @ 30/-	300: -: -
19.	— Do. — 100 Ordinary Shares @ 35/-	175: -p -
20.	Millar's Timber & Trading Company Ltd. Pinners Hall, London 100 Pref. Shares £1 each @15/-	75: -: -
21.	Selfridge Company Limited 200 Cumulative Preference Shares £1 each @ 23/1½	231: 5: -
22.	— Do. — 100 Preferred Ordinary Shares £1 each @ 26/-	130: -: -
23.	The Main Colliery Company Limited 100 Preference Shares of £1 each @ 17/6	87:10: -
24.	Celtic Collieries Limited 200 7% Cumulative Preference Shares 10/- each @ 8/6	85: -: -
25.	D. Davies & Sons Limited 100 Ordinary Shares 5/- each @ 6/-	30: -: -
26.	The General Electric Company Limited 100 6½%. Preference Shares @ 22/-	110: -: -
27.	Van Den Berghs Limited 20 6% Preference Shares £5 each @ £5	100: -: -
28.	Chinese Government £100 Bearer Bond No. 7101 8% Ten year Sterling Treasury Notes 1925/29	70: -: -
29.	Niger Company Limited £100 Bond No. 5835 Seven year Notes 8%	103: -: -
30./		

29

30.	W.H. Dorman & Company, Stafford £100 Participating Seven year Note 8% No. D695.	70	-	-
31.	United Steel Company Limited £500 'A' Debentures @ £95	475	-	-
32.	Anglo-Argentine Tramways Company Limited £600 5% Debenture Stock @ £80.	480	-	-
33.	British Dyestuffs Corporation Limited 100 Preferred Ordinary Shares @ 5/-	25	-	-
34.	Norths Navagation Collieries (1889) Limited, Cardiff 200 Ordinary Shares 5/- each @ 6/-.	60	-	-
35.	English Margarine Works (1919) Limited 100 7% Cumulative Participating Preference Shares @ 14/-	70	-	-
36.	Alliance Film Corporation Limited 50 10% Participating Preferred Ordinary Shares £1 each In liquidation value nil.	-	-	-
37.	Western Counties Shipping Company Limited 50 shares value nil.	-	-	-
38.	Marling & Evans Limited 100 Shares @ 8/3.	41	5	-
39.	Odhams Press Limited 100 8% Cumulative Preference Shares @ 12/-	60	-	-
40.	Harper Bean Limited 200 Preference shares at 3/-	30	-	-
41.	British Cellulose & Chemical Manufacturing Company Limited 200 7½% Cumulative Participating Preference Shares @ 7/6.	75	-	-
42.	Crosses & Winkworth Consolidated Mills Limited 300 Preference Shares @ 15/-	225	-	-
43.	Sheffield Steel Products Limited 50 Ordinary Shares @ 1/-	2	10	-
44.	—— Do. —— 100 Preference Shares @ 2/6	12	10	-
45.	Mieros Collieries Limited Cardiff, 100 7½% Cumulative Preference Shares @ 16/-.	80	-	-
46.	The Ebbw Vale Steel, Iron & Coal Company Limited 200 Ordinary Shares £1 each @ 13/-	130	-	-
47.	John Wood & Brothers (1920) Limited, Cotton Spinners &c., Glossop 100 8% Cumulative Participating Preference shares @ 11/-	55	-	-
48.	Edison Swan Electric Company Limited 100 Ordinary Shares @ 3/-	15	-	-
49.	Nobel Industries Limited 200 Ordinary Shares @ 16/-	160	-	-
50.	—— Do. —— 200 6% Cumulative Preference Shares @ 18/3.	176	5	-
51.	United Strips & Bar Mills Limited 100 8% Guaranteed Cumulative Preference Shares @ 18/6	92	10	-
52.	Burmah Oil Company Limited - 60 8% Cumulative Preference shares @ 26/-.	78	-	-
53./				

53.	United Steel Companies Limited £200 6% Cumulative Preference Shares @ 14/6	145	–	–
54.	Dunlop Rubber Company Limited £300 8% Debenture Stock @ £102	306	–	–
55.	Magadi Soda Company Limited £100 Debenture 6%	60	–	–
56.	The Mond Nicel Company Limited £200 Mortgage Debenture 8% Stock @ £110.	220	–	–
57.	Anglo Persian Oil Company Limited £250 8% Cumulative First Preference Shares @ 25/-	312	10	–
58.	Joshua Hoyle & Sons Limited £100 7% First Mortgage Debenture Stock.	103	15	–
59.	Mexican Eagle Oil Company Limited 500 7% Cumulative First Preference Shares @ 18/6	462	10	–
60.	Prudential Assurance Company Limited Policy No. 1107415 p. £200 and profits.	256	–	–
61.	Sum on Account Current with the London Joint City & Midland Bank, Neath Branch.	253	15	6
62.	Money and effects belonging to deceased in hands of the Officer, Board of Trade, Briton Ferry, Neath Wales, value not known, but say.	15	–	–
	Total amount of the Personal Estate. £	7390	17	8

31

AT Crarae, Lochfyne , the eleventh day of November
Nineteen Hundred and twenty two.

IN PRESENCE OF Robert Sutherland Corrigall, Solicitor, Duncon, One of
His Majesty's Justices of the Peace for the County of Argyll:
Appeared Mrs Bessie McCorquodale or Sinclair, woodside, Crarae, Lochfyne,
(wife of John Sinclair);

who, being solemnly sworn and examined, Depones: That the said Robert McCorquodale,
Master Mariner, late of Crarae, Lochfyne,
died at The Civil Hospital Ghent 'Belgium, upon the Tenth
day of October Nineteen Hundred and twenty two,
domiciled in the County of Argyll in Scotland.

That the Deponent is the Executrix nominate of the said deceased appointed
by his Last Will and Testament dated Seventh February Nineteen hun -
dred and sixteen, which is herewith produced and is signed by the
Deponent and the said Justice of the Peace as relative hereto:

That the Deponent has entered, or is about to enter, upon the possession and management
of the deceased's Estate as Execut rix foresaid, along with the said

That the Deponent does not know of any testamentary settlement or writing relative to
the disposal of the Deceased's Personal or Moveable Estate or Effects, or any part thereof, other
than the before mentioned Last Will and Testament:

That the foregoing Inventory, signed by the Deponent and the said Justice of the Peace

is a full and complete Inventory of the Personal or Moveable Estate and Effects of the said
Deceased, wheresoever situated, and belonging or due to him beneficially at the time of h is
death, in so far as the same has come to the Deponent's knowledge.

That the amount of Estate Duty (and interest thereon) payable upon this Inventory, as
particularly shewn in the Statement for Estate Duty and Summary annexed hereto, is now to
be paid to the Commissioners of Inland Revenue.

That Confirmation of the Personal or Moveable Estate in the United Kingdom,
amounting in value to £7390:17: 8
is required.

All which is truth, as the Deponent shall answer to God.

(Signed) BESSIE SINCLAIR.

R.S. CORRIGALL. J.P.

Collated by

76.

Amount of foregoing Inventory		£ 7390:17	8
„ of Debts and Funeral Expenses		81: 2	8
		£ 7309:15	—

Value of Heritage   £

Debts on Heritage

£ 7309:15 : —

Rate of Duty   4%

Net Estate Duty paid .   £ 292: 7 : 10

Interest   1 : 2 : 4

£ 293 : 10: 2

(For Settlement see Record of Wills, No. 14.)

33

Form 118 (a).

*Form for Record
Copy of Inventory
of Personal Estate
given up on Inland
Revenue Form
B-1, Small Estate.
(Testate.)*

INVENTORY

OF

THE PERSONAL ESTATE

OF

MRS. MARY WATSON OR BLUE, Widow, late of Hazelburn,
Campbeltown.

DECEASED.

AT Dunoon , the twenty eighth day of November
Nineteen Hundred and twenty two the following Inventory of the Personal
Estate of the late Mrs. Mary Watson or Blue, W

was presented for registration in this register, along with Settlement
of the deceased conform to law by Archibald Stewart,
Solicitor, Campbeltown.

Inventory of the Moveable or Personal Estate and Effects, wheresoever
situated, of the late Mrs Mary Watson or Blue, Widow, late of
Hazelburn, Campbeltown.

who died at Hazelburn aforesaid,
on the 15th day of October 19 22.

	I. SCOTLAND.	£	s.	D.
1.	Cash in house	17	14	4
2.	Household furniture and other effects in the deceased's house sold by public auction on 22nd Nov: 1922.	20	13	3
3.	£450 of 5% War Stock 1929-1947 valued at 100⅜	452	16	3
	Gross Amount of Deceased's Moveable Estate £	491	3	10

((3332) W: 2604-54 3000 413 M & G Ltd #14

BIBLIOGRAPHY

NEWSPAPERS

Belfast News Letter,
Dumfries & Galloway Standard
Dumfries & Galloway Courier.
Dumfries Times.
Dumfries Weekly Journal.
Galloway Gazette.
Galloway News.
Lloyds List & associated publications.
Wigtown Free Press.

BOOKS

British Vessels Lost At Sea (1914-1918). H.M.S.O
British Vessels Lost At Sea (1939-1945). H.M.S.O
Dictionary of Disasters at Sea during the Age of Steam. C. Hocking.
Portpatrick and its Lifeboats. . R. R. Cunningham
Edited by I. F. Macleod

ARCHIVE MATERIAL AND MISCELANEOUS SOURCES.

BelfasPublic Library
Compagnie Morbihannaise et Nantaise de Navigation, France. Department of Transport (Marine Library).
Dumfries and Galloway Regional Library (Stranraer Branch).
Guildhall Library, London.
Hogarth Shipping Co. Ltd., Glasgow.
http://www.uboat.net/index.html
http://firstworldwar.cloudworth.com/submarines-of-ww1.php.
http://www.navweaps.com
Hydrographic Department, Royal Navy.
John Kelly Ltd. Belfast (Fleet History)..
Mitchell Library, Glasgow.
M.O.D. Naval Historical Library.
National Library of Scotland, Edinburgh.
National Maritime Museum, Greenwich.
Northern Lighthouse Board.
Norwegian Maritime Museum, Oslo.
Scottish Record Office, Edinburgh (Customs & Excise Records).
The Salvage Association.
The Liverpool & Glasgow Salvage Association.
Photographs from authors collection, acquired during over forty years of research.

GLANMOR

SKEWEN

3rd Dec' 1917

J Bicknell Esq

Dear Sir

      I am very much obliged for your letter and for the kind expression of Sympathy that you convey to me from the Directors. Which I assure you I very much appreciate

      I had a very trying experience and am much grieved at the loss of all my crew; and the good old Ship "Main".

      It is now I am feeling the effects of the shock but I hope to be quite all right after a few months rest. Yours Faithfully

      R. McCorquodale

A copy of the original letter sent by Captain McCorquodale to J. Bicknell, secretary of the Main Colliery Co. This was in response to the letter sent to him from the directors of the company.

Thomas Soderstrom (Mate on the SS Main)
and his wife Annie on their wedding day.